SINGLE LADIES

MICHELE LEE

CURRENCY PRESS
The performing arts publisher

THE ACTORS' THEATRE

CURRENT THEATRE SERIES

First published in 2020
by Currency Press Pty Ltd,
PO Box 2287, Strawberry Hills, NSW, 2012, Australia
enquiries@currency.com.au
www.currency.com.au
in association with Red Stitch Theatre Company
Copyright: *Single Ladies* © Michele Lee, 2020.

COPYING FOR EDUCATIONAL PURPOSES
The Australian *Copyright Act 1968* (Act) allows a maximum of one chapter or 10% of this book, whichever is the greater, to be copied by any educational institution for its educational purposes provided that that educational institution (or the body that administers it) has given a remuneration notice to Copyright Agency (CA) under the Act.
For details of the CA licence for educational institutions contact CA, 11/66 Goulburn Street, Sydney, NSW, 2000; tel: within Australia 1800 066 844 toll free; outside Australia 61 2 9394 7600; fax: 61 2 9394 7601; email: info@copyright.com.au

COPYING FOR OTHER PURPOSES
Except as permitted under the Act, for example a fair dealing for the purposes of study, research, criticism or review, no part of this book may be reproduced, stored in a retrieval system, or transmitted in any form or by any means without prior written permission. All enquiries should be made to the publisher at the address above.
Any performance or public reading of *Single Ladies* is forbidden unless a licence has been received from the author or the author's agent. The purchase of this book in no way gives the purchaser the right to perform the play in public, whether by means of a staged production or a reading. All applications for public performance should be addressed to the author c/- Currency Press.

Typeset by Dean Nottle for Currency Press.
Cover image by Rob Blackburne, Black Photography.
Cover shows Andrea Swifte, Jem Lai and Caroline Lee.

Currency Press acknowledges the Traditional Owners of the Country on which we live and work. We pay our respects to all Aboriginal and Torres Strait Islander Elders, past and present.

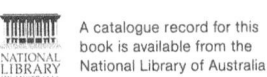
A catalogue record for this book is available from the National Library of Australia

Contents

SINGLE LADIES   1

Theatre Program at the end of the playtext

ACKNOWLEDGEMENTS

Firstly, thanks to the creative team lead by Bagryana Popov for realising the premiere production. And thanks to Red Stitch, especially Ella, for programming the work. There are also plenty of thanks for the development of the play: Creative Yarra, a program of the City of Yarra, for supporting me over three years to research and develop the play; Red Stitch for including the play in their INK development program, which enriched the development support from Creative Yarra; actors Sarah Sutherland, Jing Xuan Chan and Ra Chapman for their work on earlier developments; director Bridget Balodis for commandeering so excellently the earlier developments; dramaturg Emilie Collyer for her big and little questions and her attention to logic and detail; to my friends Django Love and Akane Kanai who critiqued my early proposals of the thematic territory of the play before it was even close to being a play; the women who spent time with me talking about what the inner city neighbourhoods mean to them now and then; and to my partner and my son, the giant and the mini, who are equally joyful and frustrating but momentous in my life.

ML

Single Ladies was first produced by Red Stitch Actors' Theatre at the Red Stitch Theatre, St Kilda, on 19 March 2020, with the following cast:

RACHEL	Jem Lai
LILIKE	Caroline Lee
ANNE	Andrea Swifte

Director, Bagryana Popov
Dramaturg, Emilie Collyer
Set and Costume Designer, Romanie Harper
Lighting Designer, Rachel Lee
Sound Designer, Elissa Goodrich
Production Manager, Greg Clarke
Stage Manager, Rain Shadrach
Assistant Stage Manager, Lowana van Dorssen

This play was developed through Red Stitch's INK writing program, proudly supported by: Cybec Foundation, Malcolm Robertson Foundation, City of Port Phillip, Copyright Australia Cultural Fund, and our Kindred.

CHARACTERS

The characters are all Australian, in the sense that they were born here or lived most of their life here in Australia.

    ANNE, of English immigrants, 70s

    LILIKE, of Hungarian immigrants, 50s; she has distinctive hair, it might be dyed blue

    RACHEL, of Chinese immigrants, 20s

They all live in Collingwood.
They are all neighbours, in fact, but don't know each other very well.

SETTING

The play pivots around the new Coles supermarket on Smith Street, Collingwood.
The play also visits the Yarra River, the windy bits that are east of Collingwood and across Hoddle Street.

TIME

The play is set over a day, give or take a few hours.
The play is set in the now, the very gentrified Collingwood.

NOTES

    / = the actor speaking the next line starts their line
    — = the actor speaking the line cuts themselves off or is cut off
    … = the actor speaking trails off

This play was written on Aboriginal country. Land was never ceded. This is, was and always will be Aboriginal land.

This play went to press before the end of rehearsals and may differ from the play as performed.

1.

It's late at night. It's dark. But we can hear the Yarra River in the background. We can see RACHEL; *she's dirty, she has a spade. She's digging.*

The sounds of the river ...

2.

The morning traffic blaring ...
And we're back at the start of the day.
LILIKE *is in her small, boxy front yard, gripping her fence. Her blue hair is alight with the morning sun. She's facing off with some suits in high-vis vests (we can't see them). They're there this morning at the empty lot across the road, which is awaiting development.*

LILIKE: —ruining this neighbourhood!
> I said fuck ya.
> You'll be paying my medical bills then. I'll send ya the bill when my head is exploding because I can't get the sight of cement out of my mind. Okay? And I mean 'you' as in Endeavour, as in the scum developers ya work for! Yep! Tell your idiot bosses that I'll take it up with council again! I'll go back to VCAT, I'll go to Melbourne Water, VicRoads, the frigging Supreme Court, till you and your application for a ten-storey car park abomination move the fuck on out of—!
> *... And the traffic blares, it's drowning her out.*

3.

It's a little later in the morning. LILIKE *is at a café, with* ANNE. *It's one of those cramped, hole-in-the-wall cafes, off Smith Street.* LILIKE *continues.*

LILIKE: —how anyone can justify paying for tea. The price of it. It's just hot water! Cafes should give tea away for free. 'Cause what's the flow-on effect? Frigging Coconut Palms! Twenty years they've been on Smith Street, ya always got the green tea for free, *always*, and now what? Now Coconut Palms, with their lemongrass chicken and their pho and their plastic tablecloths, charge for their frigging tea! They had to keep up with these prissy places. These cafes are a frigging blight on society!

ANNE: All of them?

LILIKE: Precisely. The names of these places ... Arrogant. They're *pretend*-nostalgic—'Harriet' or ... something.

ANNE: I was going to pay for your tea, if that's the issue.

LILIKE: I never tip.

ANNE: You can order something to eat too. Sometimes I get the banana bread. Not often. I have bad cholesterol.

LILIKE: Me too.

ANNE: Do you take statins?

LILIKE: They're not effective.

ANNE: Oh, you watched that report on the ABC?

LILIKE: No.

ANNE: Statins help me. If you're a pensioner, most prescriptions are quite affordable. It's convenient that there's a Chemist Warehouse on/ Smith Street—

LILIKE: Oh yeah, I know all about Chemist Warehouse. *Cancer* Warehouse.

ANNE: Pardon?

LILIKE: Like a cancer, they spread, one opening up every week. They boast about that in the PR they do. Meanwhile Mr or Mrs Pharmacist Joe or Josephine Bloggs-a-lopoulus can't compete—

ANNE: Are the pharmacists Greek around here?

LILIKE: Not anymore!

They sit.

LILIKE *might drink her tea. It's probably a very good cuppa but she finds herself obliged to find the tea offensive.*

[*Loud, so she can be heard*] Arrogant!

No-one notices her.

They sit.

ANNE: About Puckle.

LILIKE: I'm all frigging ears!

ANNE: I know her owner, I know Lizzie. We've become friends.

LILIKE: In what way?
ANNE: [*confused*] In the way where we you get to know each other—
LILIKE: Ya took Lizzie out, took her here, bought her this tea, some cake?
ANNE: I did, in fact.
LILIKE: Ya did? Ya took a homeless person *here*?
ANNE: I asked a woman *experiencing* homelessness/ to have a coffee with me here—
LILIKE: [*continuing*] Just plucked her off Smith Street?
ANNE: Well, I wouldn't say I 'plucked' her. You know how Coles does those specials on the roast chickens? I'd buy them for Lizzie and Puckle. One time we were chatting, it was cold, there was a wind, and I suggested—I said, well, why don't we get a coffee, I'll shout. We came here and she was giving me the rundown on how the kitchen works. Lizzie used to work in cafes, you see. She taught me a trick, she told me I should keep the bones from the roast chickens and then make stock, add in Vegemite at the end.
LILIKE: Well, newsflash, it's got umami.
ANNE: I had no idea about 'umami'.
> *Pause.*

LILIKE: What am I doing here?
ANNE: Discussing Puckle.
LILIKE: No, but what am I doing? In here. I reject this place and every other one. It's not just a philosophical objection. I can't eat out as much.
ANNE: You don't like the food in cafes?
LILIKE: I got peculiar taste buds nowadays.
ANNE: Peculiar in what way?
LILIKE: Just peculiar.
ANNE: Oh. You prefer ethnic foods?
LILIKE: No! 'Ethnic'—what does that mean?
ANNE: As in, say, that Coconut Palms restaurant, or that African one …
LILIKE: I'm Hungarian, d'you know that?
ANNE: No, how would I know/ that?
LILIKE: Hungarian via Yugoslavia via Collingwood. Am I ethnic?
ANNE: I suppose you might be.
LILIKE: I might be?

ANNE: I don't mean to be rude. I don't know the answer. You put me on the spot.

LILIKE: *I* put you on the spot? *You* asked *me* here. And can I just add, it is very cramped. These seats barely fit into this—what is this, an alcove?

ANNE: I think of it like a sunny reading nook. I often see people reading books here.

LILIKE: It's cramped. My foot's gone to sleep.

ANNE: Oh, did you want to move?

LILIKE: No, all good.

ANNE: I did say it could be any place of your choice.

LILIKE: I don't give a frog's fart about tea or banana bread, it doesn't matter where we're meeting. Really I should've just met ya in the Coles/ and saved ya the walk—

ANNE: Well, did you want to meet/ in the Coles then?

LILIKE: Except I'm banned from the Coles.

ANNE: In what way—What for?

LILIKE: In the way where the security guard will chuck me out. Not that it's private property, really.

ANNE: Oh, you were the lady who/ did that—

LILIKE: Yeah yeah, the nude shop.

ANNE: Are you some sort of artist?

LILIKE: No.

ANNE: I think, as far as supermarkets go, it's a very good one.

LILIKE: It's frigging Coles!

ANNE: They have that tapas bar.

LILIKE: Oh, please. Just stop it, right now. This is so bleak! Ya used to get mugged around here. In the seventies, and the eighties. Even into the nineties. All types. The Aboriginals. The Serbians. Punks. Skips. You'd just punch on.

ANNE: It's tough still.

LILIKE: A poodle hairdresser just opened up on Napier Street!

It's very bleak for LILIKE.

Pause. ANNE *is watching her.*

ANNE: Did you notice how one of Puckle's eyes is green and the other one is blue? But then in the evenings, they seem to both go grey. Don't they? I had Puckle upstairs in the community gardens for most of the daytime. We'd take walks at dusk. And then she'd go back up overnight to sleep. She was enjoying it up there, in the gardens.

LILIKE: Oh, *those* rooftop gardens, I know about them.

ANNE: You do?

LILIKE: Those developers couldn't stop raving on about them. That poncy little showroom they had next to Friends of the Earth. As if ya can manufacture a 'community' garden!

Pause.

ANNE: It's true, no-one really utilises it.

LILIKE: I knew it!

ANNE: I've taken over three plots and no-one's said anything.

Pause.

LILIKE: How many bedrooms? In your apartment?

Pause.

ANNE: One and a half.

LILIKE: And a half?

Pause.

ANNE: It's a funny shape.

LILIKE: Oh, I know the ones. I looked at those ones.

ANNE: You were interested in buying?

LILIKE: Research. Checking out what sort of prison cells they were putting into that monstrosity.

ANNE: It's not *that* bad.

LILIKE: What's worse is that car park that's going up. Ten storeys!

ANNE: People need places to park.

LILIKE: Ride a goddamn bicycle!

ANNE: I had four acres before this. Trust me, I know what it means to have a lot of space. But, well, I looked at the apartments, off the plan, and thought, 'It's about time for something small. I could be lonely here.'

Pause.

LILIKE: And are ya?

ANNE: Am I what?

LILIKE: Lonely up there?

ANNE: I have a very active online dating life.
>
> *Pause.*

LILIKE: Puckle's in my courtyard. Plenty of space, plenty of trees.
ANNE: What are you feeding her?
LILIKE: Food.
ANNE: What sort of food?
LILIKE: Oh, a dozen of those Coles roast chooks each day.
ANNE: Please don't joke—!
LILIKE: Look at ya! Ya think I can't keep a dog alive?
ANNE: Well, there's no harm in asking basic questions about her welfare—
LILIKE: Ya booked Puckle in yet at that poodle place?
ANNE: What? What on earth are you talking about—?
LILIKE: She's not good enough for it then? Thought ol' Lizzie'd entrusted you with Puckle—
ANNE: So you *did* hear me explain the situation—
LILIKE: Of course I frigging heard ya—
ANNE: Well, it didn't seem as though you understood—
LILIKE: Crystal clear, mate—!
ANNE: Because you'd abducted Puckle and you kept jogging away—
LILIKE: 'Abducted'—?!
ANNE: I'd gone inside the Westpac, briefly, I left Puckle *tied up!* on her lead—
LILIKE: As if Lizzie's coming back! She's a junkie. Probably pissed off to Springvale. Following the next hit.
ANNE: What makes you think she was using heroin?
LILIKE: Well, she wasn't doing six a.m. yoga, drinking green juice thingies, was she?
ANNE: It was prescription medicines. And she's getting clean. It's a bloody hard thing to do.
LILIKE: Ya speaking from experience?
ANNE: In a way.
>
> *Pause.*

LILIKE: What happens when Puckle starts to whine? Up there in your gardens? When it's too hot? When Lizzie stops answering your calls? When your body corporate gets onto it? When it gets too hard? You'll dump Puckle at the pound!

ANNE: I—I just, I have to say it. Because you're acting very outraged. But you live in a nice house. I know it. That fancy terrace house. I've seen you come in and out of it.
LILIKE: Oh, ya have, have ya?
ANNE: You're not like Lizzie, you're not hard done by.
LILIKE: I'm not, am I?
ANNE: I've seen people there fixing up your fence. And those gardeners who come every fortnight to tidy up the front.
LILIKE: Not every fortnight.
ANNE: It was for a few months.
LILIKE: Two months. That's all.
ANNE: Are you wealthy?
LILIKE: None of your beeswax!
ANNE: Well, I suspect you have a very romantic notion of the way things used to be.
LILIKE: I'm not wealthy. I don't own that place, I should have, but my brother bought me out and, gee ain't life ironic, I've been back there, renting at mates' rates. Except he's just sold, so looks like all that tarting up he did paid off. A fat barrister from Kew is moving in. And then off into the sunset I march.
ANNE: Where will you go?
LILIKE: The sunset. Oh, I'm romantic.

Pause.

He's one of those wiry types. He's not fat at all. The barrister.

They sit.

Quiet.

Go on. Buy me another cuppa. Then we'll go back to my joint.
ANNE: Do you mean—? Oh, my goodness! Thank you. You'll give Puckle back?
LILIKE: [*mimicking*] 'You'll give Puckle back?'
ANNE: [*about the mimicking*] Why are you/ doing that—?
LILIKE: Plenty of other people would've ignored ya, wouldn't have believed ya.
ANNE: Well … sorry? I'm confused. Are you saying—you don't want me to keep her?

LILIKE: For God's sake, whaddya think—of course I'm giving ya back the frigging dog. I'll swap ya for one of your statins. Spike me.

4.

And back to night again. It's dark. But we can hear the Yarra River, Hoddle Street in the background. We see RACHEL, *as before. Digging. Sweating.*

And now we see that LILIKE *is there too, actually. She's singing. A mournful song, sung in Hungarian. Darkness.*

RACHEL: What is that? I don't recognise the language … What is it—?

LILIKE: Oh, y'know, Rachel, just an ancient Hungarian folk song my weathered ancestors would sing as they spun wool and cured goat meat for the harsh Slavic winters.

RACHEL: Lil, it's beautiful.

LILIKE: I'm kidding. It was the jingle for an ad. They used to play it when I was a kid in Yugoslavia. It's for packet custard. From Russia. Keep digging.

LILIKE *keeps singing. The shovels and the song merge.*

5.

And then back to the daytime. Silence. At LILIKE*'s place, in her courtyard,* ANNE *and* LILIKE *are staring at the hole in* LILIKE*'s fence, which leads to an alleyway.*

LILIKE: Puckle! Come here, girl. Come on! Come to Lil.

Goddammit! Those bloody tradies! This is just—look at this shoddy work. Gaps everywhere.

Puckle! Come on, girl!

ANNE: She's not here, Lil—

LILIKE: My goddamned brother, cutting corners. She must've jumped right through that crack!

ANNE: You didn't check on her this morning?

LILIKE: This is *my* fault now?

ANNE: No, I—

LILIKE: Well, ya seem to be implying that/ I—

ANNE: I'm not implying/ anything—

LILIKE: Because I didn't hire them./ My brother did—
ANNE: The best tradies are usually the ones who can't speak any English. They know they have to work twice as hard.
LILIKE: Racist.
ANNE: Excuse me? I have a lot of ethnic/ friends—
LILIKE: Here we go. 'Some of my best friends are ethnic/ gay' et cetera et cetera.
ANNE: I won't stand here/ and be lectured at.
LILIKE: 'Some of my best friends are homeless too.'
ANNE: I didn't say 'best friends'. I was—I got to know her, I helped her—
LILIKE: Exactly! See, the problem is well-meaning people just wanting to 'help'. But only when it suits them!
ANNE: Hey! Enough! Here you are judging me, and why? I haven't done anything wrong—!
LILIKE: Yes, yes. You're a nice lady. Housing lost dogs, feeding the homeless.
ANNE: 'People experiencing homelessness', that's what you say/ that's how you speak about them—
LILIKE: Puckle! Come on, girl!
ANNE: Lil! She's not here.
LILIKE: Might be at the river. When I took her for a walk the other day, she pulled me in that direction. Sat on her hind legs, sat at the banks and just keened.
ANNE: She did?
LILIKE: Filthy part of the river too.

    Pause.

    Sorry.
ANNE: About …?
LILIKE: My general disposition. I fly off the handle sometimes.

    Pause.

ANNE: I thought you might be one of those hoarders who rescues animals.
LILIKE: What?
ANNE: When I came into your house, I was expecting …
LILIKE: Oh, right. Stacks of newspapers, thirty cats, an aviary, a family of llamas.

ANNE: I thought you'd have knick-knacks at least. Clutter.
LILIKE: Can't stand having to clean.
ANNE: I didn't expect … I don't know how you'd describe it … Is it religious?
LILIKE: Ya looked in my shrine room?
ANNE: Oh, it's a 'shrine room'—?
LILIKE: Yes, there's a huge frigging shrine in there, so it's my shrine room, and what the hell were ya doing looking inside/ there—?
ANNE: I—well, the door was open, that's all—
LILIKE: Ya bloody snoop—!
ANNE: Sorry. It caught my eye.
LILIKE: It's not religious.
ANNE: What is it?
LILIKE: A shrine to friendship.
ANNE: Have you got a large number of friends?
LILIKE: No.

    ANNE's *phone rings.*

    You can answer that.
ANNE: It's fine.
LILIKE: [*looking at* ANNE's *phone*] Who's Daniel?
ANNE: What—?
LILIKE: It's coming up as 'Daniel' on your phone.
ANNE: Please don't look at my phone.
LILIKE: Is he family?
ANNE: No.
LILIKE: Pfft. My brother's like that. Always ringing at the wrong time.
ANNE: [*cancelling the call, under her breath*] Not now.
LILIKE: Oh! Your husband?
ANNE: I don't have a husband.
LILIKE: Oh, that's right. Ya said you were dating. Oh! Your boyfriend!
ANNE: He's not my boyfriend.
LILIKE: Okay then, your sex partner—
ANNE: It's very complicated!
LILIKE: [*reading over* ANNE's *shoulder, as a message pops up*] 'What STD do you think you have?' Anne. Ya don't practise safe sex?
ANNE: I—! Don't! Stop looking at/ my messages.

LILIKE: [*looking*] Oh! Another one!
ANNE: Just—please. Stand over there.
LILIKE: [*but she's reading*] 'I don't care. We can work this out.' He's good. Anne, ya don't get that sort of reaction from many blokes.
ANNE: I know he's good—!
LILIKE: Ya gonna text him back?
ANNE: I—I ... I'm not sure what STD it might be. I have my appointment later at the health centre.
LILIKE: I'll come.
ANNE: No!

    ANNE *is sort of paralysed.*

LILIKE: Well, ya don't get to be our vintage without a few kicks up the fanny, right? I used to run that health centre, more or less. Until I got sacked. The Pygmy Devil Woman otherwise known as the Director of the health centre felt that I was unable to serve the organisation's 'new strategic direction'. That's it, in a corporate nutshell. Got my marching orders six months ago. In front of everyone. And no-one had the guts to stand up for me, to fight the changes. So I was fuming, came back here, and then y'know what I did?
ANNE: What?
LILIKE: The mirrors! Tore them all down. Tore off my clothes. And there I was starkers, staring at blank walls. And I was outta milk, I thought, 'Coles. Coles. That's where I need to go. All that milk wars business they're at the root of, they deserve a piece of me.' So I went in there with a glass bottle and asked for it to be refilled. Knowing full well they don't do that. And I was still naked, of course. But y'know what? At first, it's like I was invisible. There I was, my tits bared to the world, my stomach, my thighs, and my little scraggly pile of pubic hair. I suddenly realised: everyone in this neighbourhood is about half my age! They couldn't see me, didn't have a word for someone like me.
ANNE: Did anyone come over to you?
LILIKE: Course they did, eventually. Store manager called the coppers in. I thought, 'Great! Arrest me! I'm up for a big fight!' But the sergeant thought I was some whack job. Thought I'd done a runner from the inpatient unit up at St Vinnies!

They banned me. But it's a pity ban.
That was a shit day, Anne. A shit day for giving a shit.
Quiet.
ANNE *has relaxed again.*
ANNE: Let's go to Coles. Break the ban. We'll see if Puckle's gone back there.

6.

Still daytime. In her apartment, one of the ones above Coles, a very buzzy RACHEL *is on the phone.*

RACHEL: Em! Get this: I've discovered that the thirty-dollar pad Thai is ... a complete sham! Yup. As I was using the ladies last night, I walked past the kitchen and I see I see one of those sous chefs, he's ... I can't get over it, you'll never believe this, but yeah yeah, he pours sauce from a packet, onto the noodles! I think he was trying to be secretive? Maybe? Like it wasn't branded 'Maggi seasoning' or anything, but ... it came out of a packet. So, yeah, FYI, do *not* order that thirty-dollar Pad Thai again!

She laughs a lot, too much.

That's a hot tip from me, your local Uber Eats driver.

I ... Look, can you please, yeah, call me back when you get this?

She hangs up.

She dials again.

Em, I killed a dog. The staffy. I hit it. Last night, I was Ubering, the Uber app was going mental, and I was thinking maybe the customer's changed their order, maybe they—they hate me, or something, I don't know, yeah, I know you hate it when I jump to self-loathing conclusions—

God. It was so awful. The sound the car made, hitting that dog.

I put the dog—the body ... I put it in the boot. I put a dead dog in my boot.

Em, help!

She hangs up.

This time she's pretty worked up and takes a moment to try to calm down.

She dials again.

I just meant to say too, there's a flash sale all-day at Messina. They're doing all their botanical gelatos at half price. I know you like their coriander flavour.
Okay, Em.
Well ...
'Bye.
She hangs up.
She sobs.

7.

Sunlight. Daytime still. LILIKE *and* ANNE *are walking towards the Coles. But they're halted by* RACHEL, *who's highly frazzled and buoyed by a sudden rush of vitriol.*

RACHEL: [*seizing upon* LILIKE, *shouting*] You! Lilike Kovacs! Fucking bitch!
LILIKE: Ah?
RACHEL: [*shouting*] Fucking psycho!
LILIKE: Excuse/ me?
RACHEL: Do you remember me? Huh? Lilike?
LILIKE: No, got no idea who you are—
ANNE: We're just visiting Coles, that's all.
RACHEL: [*to* LILIKE, *shouting*] You crazy bitch!
ANNE: Stop that—!
RACHEL: Don't tell me to/ stop—
ANNE: Stop that, stop using that awful language. Swearing. Accosting. Yelling. That is *no* way to speak to another person—
LILIKE: [*to* ANNE] Go, Anne!
ANNE: [*continuing*] Who do you think you are?
RACHEL: Who do you think *you* are?
ANNE: I'm Anne Robertson. I live upstairs, I shop inside there—
RACHEL: I'm Rachel Wong and I fucking live upstairs too—
ANNE: Stop that. Stop swearing. Now!

Beat.

LILIKE: Oh oh oh oh oh! Anne! I remember! She's one of the project managers from the developers! From Endeavour! For the car park. Ten storeys!

RACHEL: Exactly! A fucking car park. One tiny fucking/ car park. That's all!

ANNE: All this swearing!

RACHEL: [*shouting*] I don't care!

LILIKE: [*to* ANNE] She looks very different now—

RACHEL: I lost a lot of weight—!

LILIKE: [*to* ANNE] They're building car parks all over Melbourne, they start with their small-development car parks, test the waters—

RACHEL: I lost my job because of you.

Beat.

I don't work with Endeavour anymore.

LILIKE: And how is that *my* doing?

RACHEL: Because because …

LILIKE: Spit it out.

RACHEL: Because the way I handled public stakeholders was apparently consistently below the standard for handling public stakeholders! The 'public', in my case, was you. I couldn't handle you! And now I'm an unemployed loser who buys packet curry from Coles and eats them cold in the car as she does Uber Eats.

Beat.

ANNE: Let's move over here. The door keeps opening and closing. It's annoying.

They all move.

[*To* RACHEL] You're on level three? With your girlfriend? I'm on the first floor. I post a lot on the Facebook page. You and your—what's your girlfriend's name?

RACHEL: Emily.

ANNE: Why don't you come along to the barbecue next week? On the patio?

RACHEL: We're not …

ANNE: Check with Emily?

At the mention of Emily again, RACHEL *can't help it, she erupts, she sobs.* ANNE *is immediately concerned,* LILIKE *a little baffled.*

Rachel?

A moment.

Rachel? What's the matter?

But RACHEL *sobs even more.*

[*To* LILIKE] Is this about the car park?

LILIKE: [*to* RACHEL] Is this about the time I came to your offices? [*To* ANNE] I wore this weird costume, caused havoc. Nothing traumatic, but she was uppity.

RACHEL *keeps sobbing.*

ANNE: Would you like—do you need a hug?

RACHEL: No—my God, I don't even know you.

ANNE: I'm sorry, I—I just thought …

LILIKE: Have ya seen a dog?

RACHEL: What?

LILIKE: A dog.

RACHEL: What sort of dog?

LILIKE: Her name is Puckle. Staffy—

RACHEL: [*with a sinking feeling*] Um?

LILIKE: Quite dark, with a grey chest.

ANNE: Lizzie—that's Puckle's owner. She used to sit here, very chatty, if you gave her half a minute. Both of them, they were here all the time.

LILIKE: Best seat in the house if you're after spare change.

RACHEL: I haven't seen them recently … I haven't been getting out much …

ANNE: Oh, Puckle! I'm almost tempted to run in, buy a chicken, carry it around and just … pray she whiffs the scent of it. Now what, Lil? Roam the streets all day?

LILIKE: Actually! Yes! Basic search party protocol. Posters for Puckle. On every street!

As the Coles doors open and shut, LILIKE *looks in, addressing an unseen security guard.*

That's right, it's the old bird who came in starkers.

And then, in an impetuous moment, LILIKE *lifts her top and flashes the Coles.*

No response really, the doors open and shut.

A moment.

He's barely even looking. Bloody new security guards.

RACHEL *is kind of dumbstruck, staring at* LILIKE. LILIKE *pulls her top down.*

ANNE: [*to* RACHEL] We could use the help. Will you come?
LILIKE: [*to* ANNE] Pfft. She won't be any help—
RACHEL: I'm so so *not* going anywhere with—

8.

And RACHEL *is shoe-horned awkwardly into a little gap in a crowd on the 86 tram, wishing she was invisible.* ANNE *and* LILIKE *stand next to her, hemming her in. It's very crowded at this time of day. There must've been a delay on the previous trams. You could potentially have the tram dinging and the prerecorded announcer saying, 'Folks, a reminder that this is an 86D, we'll be terminating at the depot. For now, your next stop is Alexandra Parade'. Which then takes them to ...*

9.

Officeworks. The photocopiers are humming. ANNE *and* LILIKE *are leaning over the counter, hand-writing a 'missing dog' poster.* RACHEL *is scrolling on her phone, still wishing herself silently into oblivion.*

ANNE: Do you think we might—?
LILIKE: What—?
ANNE: Write our phone numbers again a little larger—
LILIKE: They *are* large—
ANNE: The spacing's cramped—
LILIKE: There's plenty of space, ya could build a car park between them! [*Looking at* RACHEL *for a reaction*] Where's the sense of humour?
ANNE: Is that a one or a seven?
LILIKE: It's a— [*Looking more closely*] Well, fine. Fine. I would've written the numbers bigger if there wasn't so much bloody text! It's a missing dog poster, not *War and Peace*.

ANNE: I *did* suggest you summarise what I was saying—
LILIKE: Can barely concentrate, can I? Standing over my bloody shoulder!/
ANNE: Because I don't have my glasses with me because you rushed us down here—
LILIKE: [*looking at* RACHEL, *about* ANNE] She's been micro-managing me, hasn't she?
RACHEL: [*distracted*] What, sorry?
LILIKE: Get off your bloody phone!
RACHEL: Sorry, but I'm/ just—
LILIKE: We're working here—
RACHEL: Yeah, I'm working too, sorry. Or trying to. I should be out there.
LILIKE: If someone wants a burger, they can walk to it. Get us another piece of paper. Come on!
RACHEL: Um, which sort of paper exactly …?
LILIKE: *This* paper. In A3. This exact one we got in aisle seven.
ANNE: [*to* LILIKE] I'll get the paper, it's fine.
LILIKE: Don't be ridiculous. Rachel—get the paper.
ANNE: Leave her alone, Lil! She's fragile—
LILIKE: She needs firm direction—
RACHEL: You guys could just make the poster on your phone? Then you wouldn't need to write it up onto paper.
LILIKE: [*dismissively*] What? Pfft. That *might* work—
ANNE: Rachel! What a fantastic idea!
RACHEL: [*embarrassed*] Thank you.
LILIKE: [*mimicking*] 'Thank you.'
ANNE: [*to* RACHEL] Ignore her. [*To both of them*] I have pictures of Puckle. We'll insert them onto the posters, and we'll have to print them in colour—
LILIKE: And how much is that going to cost, moneybags?
ANNE: It doesn't matter. [*Getting out her phone*] How on earth will people know what dog we're talking about unless we use a picture—?
LILIKE: Fine. Pick a few, I'll make the final call.
ANNE: [*continuing*] It was frankly criminal the way people wouldn't smile at Puckle, wouldn't even say hello to Lizzie.
RACHEL: Well, I guess when 'people' walked by, they weren't, yeah, ignoring them as a personal thing. We've all got our own problems to deal with, yeah?

ANNE: [*searching on her phone*] It's exactly those attitudes that make us all so alone.
LILIKE: [*watching* ANNE *search*] You're rubbish with your phone. Look in the photos section. Not your messages.
ANNE: I've got a beautiful set of photos inside one of my messages. I sent them to my son.
RACHEL: It's great that you guys are—well, that *we're* making these posters to find Puckle. But don't you think that there's a really high chance that Puckle's probably just ... left?
LILIKE: Just hopped on the bus? For a little doggy sightseeing?
RACHEL: Well well well, sorry, but Puckle *is* a dog, she doesn't need a bus to get around. She might have, yeah, got spooked and ran off. And then, well, it's busy around here, a lot of traffic in small streets and the lighting at night is awful, and maybe ... maybe Puckle was freaking out and she wasn't doing her dog intuition thing and maybe she ran out and hit a car—
LILIKE: Dogs don't 'hit' moving cars.
RACHEL: I'm just putting it out there! [*More to herself*] Shit! Is it illegal to hit a dog—?
ANNE: Oh, Puckle! She did get jittery.
RACHEL: [*more to herself*] Was Puckle even registered? Microchipped?
LILIKE: [*to* ANNE] Finally! She's talking sense now! We get the microchip number, get the vet to look it up on their database, get a real location on Puckle!
ANNE: I've got no idea if Lizzie took Puckle to a vet—
LILIKE: Doesn't matter! We'll go door-knocking at the local vets, we'll ask around.
ANNE: [*showing* RACHEL *the phone*] Look. Puckle.
RACHEL: [*looking, sickened at seeing Puckle*] Oh God, oh God. Anne, could you—I wouldn't mind that hug now? Please? Please?
ANNE: Oh. Of course.

She hugs RACHEL *as* LILIKE *watches.*

The hug actually lingers. It feels quite good.

LILIKE: Well. Don't expect me to join in.
ANNE: [*to* RACHEL] A good hug helps with a bad day, doesn't it?
LILIKE: What helps with a bad day is the minimum wage, a safety net.

ANNE *and* RACHEL *stop hugging.*

There's been real tenderness, actually. ANNE *is feeling emotional.*

ANNE: Is this the definition of a needle in a haystack? Putting up a few posters? Calling around vets? Puckle could be anywhere now.

Beat.

My spare room. I never offered it. I could have been Lizzie's safety net.

LILIKE: What? Ya think ya should be responsible for every junkie?

ANNE: For God's sake, I told you already, don't throw around that word: 'junkie'.

RACHEL: [*genuine*] So Lizzie *wasn't* a junkie—?

ANNE: Stop it! You're both being incredibly judgemental—!

LILIKE: [*to* RACHEL] Sensitivity is very important here. Anne used to dabble in drugs.

RACHEL: [*to* ANNE] You/ did?

LILIKE: [*to* RACHEL] Ya don't get to Anne's age without a few wayward turns.

ANNE: What on/ earth are you—?

LILIKE: What? I read the subtext before.

ANNE: It was my son. He's recovered. But I didn't help him at the time. End of story.

Beat.

LILIKE: [*who's had a good idea, shouting*] I'm a bloody genius! [*To* RACHEL] Get your phone out. [*To* ANNE] Send that Puckle picture to Rachel.

ANNE: For the poster?

LILIKE: No. Better. For the *online* aspect of our campaign! All these oily little cafes and burger joints, they all have Instagram, Facebook, Twitter. They all have thousands of little foodie fans, coming in and outta our neighbourhood. They'll have intel about Puckle's movements! That's going to quadruple the reach of our search! And Miss Millennial Chinese Lesbian Uber Eats Driver is probably all across social media!

RACHEL: Yes, but—

LILIKE: But what?

RACHEL: It's just, just—social media's crowded. Let's just stick with posters?

LILIKE: But we have digital cut-through! Puckle's face! Those eyes! That'll get them all re-posting or re-tweeting, and for the analogue folks, we'll hit them with Anne's colour posters, and then we've got a whole citizens' brigade on the hunt.
ANNE: Lil! Fantastic! [*To* RACHEL] What's your number?
LILIKE: [*to* RACHEL] Go on! Give it up! Now!

10.

And the posters are done! They are all eating much-deserved banh mi from N Lee Bakery and custard slices too.

ANNE *and* LILIKE *eat like they are the boss of everything, riding a high, as if the whole of Collingwood is at their beck and call. Maybe they're hanging up posters. Or you could have the social media message spiralling out, all over the set:*

'Attention Collingwood! Have you seen Puckle? We are her carers and it seems as though she escaped our care last night. We're desperately trying to locate her. If you have any information, please message us. Thanking you in advance.'

If there was ever to be a break-out moment for an excellent group dance routine in their lives, this would be it. For example, the radio at N Lee's could be playing 'Single Ladies' by Beyonce (this is the obvious ironic choice), and ANNE *and* LILIKE *might be compelled to celebrate with an impromptu dance.* RACHEL *is sort of just going along with things, maybe she hopes it's a bad dream that will end.*

11.

And then it's later. The bad dream isn't over for RACHEL. *She's in reception at the local community health clinic. Some of the missing Puckle posters are up.* RACHEL *is desperately making a phone call.*

RACHEL: [*on her phone*] —please please please please please, Em, please don't ignore me! Fuck! It's *not* one of those 'Rachel crying wolf' situations, okay? I know it sounds like I'm making it up but I'm stuck with these crazy ladies who are forcing me to find the dog when I have the dog and I don't know what—

LILIKE *enters, mad as a bull. Feeling sprung,* RACHEL *tries to put her phone away—*
LILIKE: [*shouting*] My God, Rachel—!
RACHEL: Um um um—yes?
LILIKE: Can you believe it—?
RACHEL: Be/lieve what, sorry?
LILIKE: [*continuing*] —the way the receptionist looked at Anne! A senior citizen is here, picking up her STI results, showing us that it's okay to look after one's sexual health *at any age*, and that little twerp couldn't hide her shock. Staff here are inept—
RACHEL: Well, I think they seem kind of busy, yeah?
LILIKE: And those tablet computer thingies? Did ya see them behind the counter—?
RACHEL: No, not really, sorry—
LILIKE: Pay attention—!
RACHEL: Sorry, it's just just I happen to be very nauseous—
LILIKE: How much did they splurge on them? Waste of money! And no frigging tea! What happened to the free tea?! Jesus! Ya leave a workplace and it all goes to the dogs.

Pause.

RACHEL: Do you think I could ask the receptionist for some Nurofen?
LILIKE: Pfft. Good luck trying.

Pause.

RACHEL: So … you used to work here?
LILIKE: Thanks for asking, and yes, I did. Once upon a time, I kept this whole place ticking over. Now look at it. Can barely stomach even walking by!
Puckle! I'm sticking it out for ya! Standing here, breathing in the same oxygen as that bloody Pygmy Director. Should give her a piece of my mind again.

Pause.

What? What's the matter with you?
RACHEL: Nothing! You're a little shouty and I just—I have bad nausea, like I said.
LILIKE: All these low-lifers around, right? Here for their freebies! Sex workers! Druggies! Ex-cons! They creep ya out!

RACHEL: Look, I don't care who else is here. It's everyone's private business here, yeah? I hate going to the doctors, you're just just just so close to everyone's issues.
LILIKE: *They're* a key target market for the posters. They all knew Puckle. How are the online aspects of the campaign? Any leads from the bourgeois gourmands?
RACHEL: No 'leads', sorry. Just a ton of messages of support.
LILIKE: Early days. [*About the posters again*] Anyway, soup kitchen's starting up soon on Stanley Street. We could do a bit of face-to-face there.

Pause.

What?
RACHEL: Nothing …
LILIKE: Well, stop looking like that.
RACHEL: I'm just looking like myself.
LILIKE: Pathetic.
RACHEL: Fuck off.
LILIKE: Why are ya letting me rile you up? Ya weren't like this at Endeavour. I mean, ya were a pain in the ass, but ya were more … switched on, ready to give tit for tat.
RACHEL: Well, it didn't work with you. I mean, the mediation, VCAT, all of it, and the yelling, you know, all of that, all of that yelling stuff. Why do you even do it?
LILIKE: What? Yelling?
RACHEL: Yes!
LILIKE: I got a lotta time right now—
RACHEL: But you won't win. Ever. They have millions of dollars, they'll fight you, they're going ahead with the car park, with the next project, and the next one. They weren't ever going to stop because you went to VCAT a couple of times—
LILIKE: Five times—
RACHEL: This isn't the movies! You're nothing. No offence.

Pause.

LILIKE: Well, ya look back on your life—on your achievements, meagre as they may seem—and the only thing that matters is the effort that ya put in. I'm not going to my grave quietly. Every day for me is the chance to yell and scream a little louder until someone pays attention. Otherwise ya might as well be dead already.

RACHEL: And what? While you do that, you just bulldoze over people like me?

LILIKE: Oi. Fact check. I wasn't the one that fired ya.

Beat.

RACHEL: Em got me the job at Endeavour. I was winging it.

LILIKE: Here's a little free careers counselling. Everyone is winging it.

Which is actually sincere, so that makes LILIKE *uncomfortable.*

Check your phone.

RACHEL: Why?

LILIKE: Just frigging check it 'cause I told you to.

RACHEL: But it's just the same messages wishing us well, et cetera et cetera.

LILIKE: Message them back. Tell them to ask their friends if they've seen Puckle.

RACHEL: There are sixty-five messages. I can't—what? Write to them all.

LILIKE: What the hell have ya been doing since I was out there?

RACHEL: I was ... I was ... Nothing, I guess. Being useless. Pathetic.

She lies down on the ground.

LILIKE *watches, bemused.*

I don't want to look at Anne. Anne's got these really ... kind eyes.

RACHEL*'s phone bings.*

Oh my God, Em?

RACHEL *checks. It's not. A little squeaky sob from* RACHEL.

LILIKE: Get up.

Nothing from RACHEL.

Look. I'll write the first twenty people back, then we'll swap. Okay?

LILIKE *takes the phone. And something catches her eye immediately.*

Rachel! This Desmond bloke. He just wrote to us.

RACHEL: What/ do you mean?

LILIKE: Jesus! Get up! Lift your game—
RACHEL: Sorry, but/ I was distracted—
LILIKE: [*reading*] 'I have your missing dog.'
RACHEL: Is he kidding—?
LILIKE: [*continuing reading*] 'How much is the reward?'
RACHEL: He must be kidding—
LILIKE: [*writing back, reading aloud as she does it*] 'No reward, mate! Just the good feeling of returning a dog to its carers!'
  [*Watching the phone*] Look! Ooh! He's writing back.
  A bing.
  [*Looking*] There she is! That's Puckle!
RACHEL: [*confused*] What?
  A bing.
LILIKE: [*reading*] 'Is this her? If so, perhaps we can negotiate on the reward?'
RACHEL: [*looking at the phone*] That could be any dog.
LILIKE: Don't be ridiculous. It's Puckle. [*About Des*] Asshole! 'Negotiate'?
RACHEL: Please don't text him back—
LILIKE: Don't worry. I'll butter him up, keep him on side until he gets here. Then I'll give him a serve. [*Texting*] 'Yes, of course we can negotiate! Let's meet asap. Please bring Puckle. Thank you.'
RACHEL: Oh god oh god oh god oh god—
  ANNE *enters.*
ANNE: It's herpes. I can't take things back, all that I can do now is to deal with the situation, and make different decisions in the future. What's done is done.
LILIKE: Some asshole's got Puckle. But this asshole is bringing us Puckle!
RACHEL: Oh God, I think the pâté might have been off.

  And RACHEL *vomits up the banh mi and the vanilla slice.*

  ANNE *and* LILIKE *stare at the mess, before* LILIKE *quickly erupts with joy.*

LILIKE: Ha! Take that, Pygmy!

12.

Night has fallen. It's ANNE*'s small, open-plan apartment. Dinner is being cooked.*

LILIKE *is riled up—is she angry, excited?* RACHEL *is on the sofa, with a blanket pulled over her. It's probably one of those nice mohair ones.*
ANNE *is upbeat. She's on the phone.*

ANNE: [*on the phone*] —asymptomatic, unfortunately. Until now.
Who knows when?
It might have been Phil. My second husband. Remember, I told you about—?
No doubt he brought things back to our bed.
Well, I am smiling. Because I can tell you're not angry. I just expected ...
Well, thank you. I appreciate that.
You'll see your doctor?
I hope you find a wife.
Thank you.
She hangs up.
Or was he the married one?
She makes another call.
[*On the phone again*] Hi. Yes, it's Anne Robertson.
I'm good. Thank you for asking. Yourself?
Look, I'm calling with awkward news./ I just went to the local clinic this afternoon and got my STI results.
Yes, that's right, 'sexually transmitted infections' is what they call them these days.

LILIKE: [*on* RACHEL*'s phone, reading aloud*] 'Bonsoir, ladies. Puckle and I will be a tad bit late for our rendezvous.' What a dickhead! It's torture, being nice to him!

ANNE: [*to* LILIKE] Quiet, please!/ [*Continuing on the phone*] Look, I'll get to the point. I have herpes—

LILIKE: [*while writing back*] Bloody—aren't these new smartphones meant to be easier to use—?

ANNE: [*continuing on the phone*] Yes, that's the—it's a virus. Most people have it in their system, in fact, they're born with it./
Well, it presents with fever, blisters.
That's right. On the outside of my vagina, on the folds.
LILIKE: [*continuing*] How do I insert one of those ha-ha winky faces? Rachel? Winky face.
RACHEL: [*under the blanket*] I don't know, just google the instructions please—
ANNE: [*continuing on the phone*] Around the anus too—
LILIKE: [*sending the text*] Wait wait, don't worry, solved it, fixed it myself! As per usual, I'm doing it all. Strategy and implementation, comms.
ANNE: [*continuing on the phone*] Yes!/
Exactly! The exact same virus as the one that gives people cold sores although this is—what I have—it's a different strain—
A bing.
LILIKE: [*reading*] 'New idea, ladies. What if we have dinner as my reward? There are plenty of restaurants on Smith Street!'
RACHEL: [*prairie-dogging up from under the blanket, shouting*] Let's do it!
ANNE: [*continuing on the phone*] Oh, I'm sorry, yes it's loud./
I've got some dinner guests here and they're having a separate conversation. What I was saying is—
Yes, that's right. Given our encounters, I really urge you to get tested too.
Yes. Even if you're not symptomatic yet.
LILIKE: [*texting back*] 'Of course, Des! Ha. Ha. Let's meet first and then we'll go from there.'
RACHEL: [*shouting*] Let's get Mexican! I love it! I love this couch!
LILIKE: [*looking at* RACHEL *oddly*] What?
RACHEL: [*back under the blanket*] Nothing. Ignore me.
ANNE: [*continuing on the phone*] Oh, goodness, that *does* sound like a busy week ahead.
[*Listening*] Busier in retirement, isn't that what they say?
Well, you'll be hard-pressed to fit a doctor's appointment in with your schedule!

[*Listening*] Oh, it's a special occasion here. We're having pumpkin soup, a main, and a dessert.
Yes. Special occasion.
Enjoy the hand-gliding. And I hope you find a wife.
Thank you.
ANNE *hangs up.*
Look. I know this is awkward for you both, me making these phone calls.
LILIKE: Hearing about herpes is music to my frigging ears!
ANNE: No-one needs to bury their heads in the sand about uncomfortable truths.
Pause.
RACHEL: Can someone close the window?
ANNE: [*moving towards it*] Why don't we just invite this Desmond fellow up for dinner?
LILIKE: Because we're being *fake* friendly.
ANNE: But why not just have him up as a matter of goodwill?
LILIKE: Ya gonna try and date him too, give him herpes?
ANNE: I just mean that there's enough soup. And he's doing us a big favour, coming here, returning Puckle. I'm not afraid to treat him like a friend.
RACHEL: Sorry, is the window closed yet, guys?
ANNE: Are you getting a cold?
RACHEL: Maybe?
LILIKE: The plan is this: he arrives, we go downstairs, tell him off, then we get Puckle—no reward offered, mate, so none given. That's it. That's the plan.
ANNE: Don't be so inflexible. He deserves a hundred dollars at the least. Give me the phone/
LILIKE: No/
ANNE: Rachel, please, take your phone back. Let's text this Desmond—
RACHEL: Lil, can I please have my phone/ back—?
LILIKE: No! I'm on comms with Des.
ANNE: [*to* RACHEL] Take it back.
LILIKE: [*scrolling, about* RACHEL] You *did* lose a lot of weight.
RACHEL: Are you—are you looking at my Facebook photos?

LILIKE: And your Instagram. [*Reading*] '*So good. Waited forty-five minutes. So worth it.*' [*Showing* ANNE] A laksa. From August.
ANNE: [*looking*] That's Em, isn't it?
LILIKE: [*scrolling*] You used to eat out a lot, didn't ya? Explains the plump.
RACHEL: Can you please—? Just just stop looking at my profile, please stop!
ANNE: [*to* RACHEL] You're a gorgeous couple.
RACHEL: I know we were! We broke up in August! Okay?
ANNE: Oh.
LILIKE: Oh.
ANNE: … I'm sorry, I didn't realise. I thought—
RACHEL: [*suddenly tossing off the blanket*] Shit. Now I feel hot. I'm hot. I can't eat soup. I can't eat it. Oh God oh God oh God—

> RACHEL *lies on the couch, exposed, eyes closed.*

ANNE: [*a little quieter*] Perhaps you shouldn't have invaded her privacy.
LILIKE: Well, don't have a Facebook account then, right?

> *Nothing from* RACHEL. *She is squeezing her eyes shut.*

ANNE: Lil …
LILIKE: It's true! People displaying all their personal information online, then expecting people not to view it. I mean, frigging hell—
ANNE: When I was talking to the nurse—
LILIKE: What nurse?
ANNE: At the health centre. I was talking about the three of us searching for Puckle, and the nurse she—well, she made quite the face when I mentioned you. So I had to ask what was going on. The 'job' you had at the health centre—
LILIKE: What about it?
ANNE: Lil.
LILIKE: What?
ANNE: You worked in government, but you got sacked for being a bully, and then I assume you couldn't find work so you went to the health centre to *volunteer* full-time, but while you were there, you upset clinicians, disclosed patient information, they had to let you go. You don't need to lie to me. I'm not judging you for feeling embarrassed.
LILIKE: I—this is frigging unbelievable! Just—who is this frigging nurse? I'll go back there, give them a serve!

SINGLE LADIES

ANNE: Calm down, Lil.
RACHEL: [*eyes still closed*] I thought you said you ran the place?
LILIKE: Oh, you do *not* get to question me, Rachel from Endeavour! So shut your mouth/!
ANNE: [*to* LILIKE] Stop yelling./ Please—
LILIKE: If ya poke this bear, expect to get yelled at—!
ANNE: You don't always have to pick a fight. [*A bit quieter, mouthing and motioning in* RACHEL'*s direction*] Especially with the weak.
RACHEL: Weak? … What?
ANNE: Um.
RACHEL: Sorry, Anne, did just call me 'weak'?
ANNE: Well, yes, but in my defence, you were crying on the footpath when we met you.
RACHEL: [*laughing hard, shouting*] What a loser, right?!

> RACHEL *laughs a lot.* ANNE *and* LILIKE *don't know what to make of it.*
>
> *A bing from* RACHEL'*s phone.* LILIKE *smiles magnanimously at* ANNE. *A change of heart.*

LILIKE: There are gnats, people who speak ill of me, e.g. that nurse, and they're the idiots who *always* underestimate me. Anne, are *you* an idiot? I suspect not! Because when ya see Puckle sitting over there in your half room, slurping her share of pumpkin soup, I think ya'll remember that I'm the one that found the needle in the haystack!

> *And now* LILIKE *reads the text. Still beaming, she goes over and opens the window. Her smile wanes as she looks down—*

ANNE: [*about the window*] I just closed that/ for Rachel—
LILIKE: [*still looking down*] Puckle's not there.
ANNE: What?
RACHEL: Why not?
LILIKE: Des says he's down there, opposite the Coles. I can't see Puckle though. Did he—must've gone to the Woolies then?

> LILIKE *writes a message.*
>
> *She waits.* ANNE *comes over and joins her.*
>
> RACHEL *burrows into herself, squeezing her eyes shut, maybe pinching herself to the point of white pain.*

A bing.

ANNE *and* LILIKE *both read.* LILIKE*'s waned smile now becomes a tight grimace.* ANNE *is confused.*

ANNE: Why is he saying/ that he won't—?

LILIKE: [*shouting*] Prick!

Beat.

RACHEL *creaks open her eyes.*

RACHEL: What's going on?

ANNE: [*to* LILIKE] Read her the message.

LILIKE: [*reading*] 'Ladies, I am definitely here. But I need to meet you first. Show me your faces. I've left Puckle in my car.'

RACHEL: He's lying! He has Puckle! He does! He must!

ANNE: Yes, and if Lil had just said a hundred dollars for a reward, upfront, that's all she had to do—

LILIKE: We've just got to go down there, don't we? Just—just confront the bastard!

ANNE: What does he look like?

LILIKE: I don't know.

ANNE: What do you mean you don't know?

RACHEL: But but, have you—didn't you check his profile?

LILIKE: Why would I check his profile?

RACHEL: Because that's what you do when someone messages you and and you don't know them, you stalk them.

LILIKE: Well, sorry to all concerned if I'm not addicted to social media like the rest of the population and not hot-wired to stalk. [*She's scrolling over his page.*] Fine. Stalking. Stalking. Not much there admittedly.

Noticing ANNE*'s and* RACHEL*'s nervous faces.*

What?

ANNE: Ask him to identify himself.

The phone starts to vibrate.

LILIKE: Why bother? He's FaceTiming us now.

RACHEL: [*timid*] Actually, FaceTime is an Apple application whereas just calling on Facebook Messenger is simply called video chatting—

LILIKE: I frigging know that!

ANNE: Lil! Stop it! All this hostility when we're all trying to assess this situation/
RACHEL: Should we just/?
ANNE: [*to* LILIKE] Answer the phone!
LILIKE: [*shouting*] Get off my case already!
ANNE: Do *not* yell at me in my own home! Answer it!

But the phone stops ringing.

The phone bings. LILIKE *checks the message. She's shattered.*

What's he saying?

Pause.

Lil?

Pause.

Lil?

LILIKE: That frigging—he just sent us a selfie. Of his *dick*—
ANNE: Why—?
RACHEL: Sh/it—
ANNE: What on earth/ is happening?
LILIKE: [*continuing*] —his shrivelled, speckled, sad, sad dick. Fucker!
RACHEL: Fuck—
ANNE: But does he have Puckle?
LILIKE: What a frigging stupid question!
RACHEL: Shit fuck shit fuck, I take it back, I take it all back, I am so sorry! I am so so so sorry!
ANNE: Oh, for God's sake, this is not about you, Rachel!

RACHEL *clams up.*

The phone again, buzzing. It keeps buzzing as ANNE *and* LILIKE *bicker.*

Who is that man downstairs? Who is he?
LILIKE: I don't know. Answer the phone and ask him yourself.
ANNE: You answer it! You're apparently on 'comms'.
LILIKE: Well, you're the phone expert, clearly, shoving all your sex confessions down our throats, the whole bloody street could hear you!
ANNE: I was being honest! I was setting an example for you, quite frankly.
LILIKE: If you're so noble then, why didn't ya call Daniel first? Why haven't ya called him yet?

ANNE: I—I was planning to, of course I was!

LILIKE: Oh, let me bow before Saint Anne, Bearer of the Herpes Confession, oh, Doler of Roast Chook to the Deprived, the Holiest of Holy Dogsitters—!

ANNE: And to think you have a 'shrine to friendship' when you clearly have an inability to *actually* make friends—

LILIKE: —but ya can't even tie a lead! Puckle was practically escaping when I found her! Answer the phone!

ANNE: You knew Des was a fake. But you wanted him to come here just so you could pick another fight, so you answer it!

The phone again, buzzing. RACHEL *now grabs it and answers it.*

RACHEL: [*on the phone, shouting*] Fuck you, Des! Okay?! So you don't have Puckle? So you tricked us? You fucking evil human being, get off the internet and don't ever FaceTime this phone again!

RACHEL *hangs up, breathless, fired up.*

LILIKE *is laughing.*

ANNE: [*turning on* LILIKE] You think this is all a joke. You're almost laughing.

LILIKE: I'm just resigned to disappointment and it no longer surprises me.

ANNE: Can't you just apologise, for fuck's sake?!

LILIKE: It's not my fault that people are dickheads! It's not my fault if people rip ya off, if they fuck ya over, if they lie, if they break their promises! It's not my fault!

Silence.

ANNE: [*to* LILIKE] Just leave. Rachel and I can find Puckle.

LILIKE: [*going to leave*] Fine.

RACHEL: No-no-no-no-wait-don't-go-sorry-guys-I-I-I-killed-Puckle!

ANNE: You—you did what?

Pause.

LILIKE: When?

Pause.

For an extended moment.

RACHEL: Last night I—I hit her last night I was Ubering last night and I hit her last night it was an accident then I—I freaked out I put her in my boot last night.

Silence.

ANNE: Show me. Show me Puckle.

13.

Down in the car park basement, by RACHEL*'s car.* ANNE, LILIKE *and* RACHEL. RACHEL *lifts the door on her boot.* ANNE *and* LILIKE *look at Puckle.*
ANNE *is devastated. She leaves.*

14.

And we're outside, back to the deep of the night, by the river, it's dark. We see RACHEL *and* LILIKE. *Dirty. They're exhausted. They put their shovels down. They sit.*

Long silence.

LILIKE: I'll fetch Anne.

    LILIKE *leaves.*

    Silence.

    RACHEL *gets out her phone and dials.*

RACHEL: [*on the phone*] Em? Did you ever want to know if it feels utterly suspicious buying three shovels from Bunnings late on a Friday night?

    Pause.

Did you get a chance to go to Messina?

    Pause.

So I'm going to chuck this phone out. And then I won't get a new one for a little while. And then, when I do, I won't call you again. Not that you were ever asking me to call you every day, but—yeah, you let me go, *so* easily. Like there wasn't even a debate about it on your end. You just … you dropped me. But I want there to be a debate. I want to be debatable.

    RACHEL *hangs up.*

    Quiet. Just the river flowing.

15.

Under the night sky, up in the community gardens, amongst the under-utilised and empty plots.

ANNE *is there in the gardens. She's been there for some time.*

LILIKE *is there too. She's dirty—after all, she's been down by the river digging a grave.*

LILIKE: We're waist-deep in dirt, river's practically lapping at our feet, and who calls? My frigging brother. Perfect timing as per frigging usual. 'Oh, Lil, lend me a hand. New owner wants to push settlement forward. Thirty days. He'll cover any inconveniences. Whaddya say?' Well, what I said was that he can bugger off. That barrister said ninety days, so ninety days it is.

ANNE: Is there anything I can do?

LILIKE: What about a time machine? Should've never let my brother buy me out.

ANNE: What about my spare room?

LILIKE: Your cupboard?

ANNE: Well, yes, I know it's small—

LILIKE: Ya can barely fit a chair in there!

ANNE: I'd clear it out of my things, and then it can fit a double bed, maybe. Definitely a single bed. Let me help you. You don't have to pay me rent.

Pause.

LILIKE: Come to the river. We've done all the digging, ya won't have to get your hands dirty.

ANNE: You think that's my issue? Dirt? Lil, I might not have many relationships intact from where I lived before. I'm not inundated with visitors right now, it's true not even my own son has asked to visit. But I wasn't afraid to get my hands dirty. I buried plenty of animals.

Pause.

LILIKE: Then bury Puckle with us.

Beat.

We're using my shrine as a gravestone.

ANNE: What? It's—Oh Lil, it's it's—

LILIKE: Crude, huge, tacky. So it's not gonna go into storage again, right?
ANNE: You'll just leave it on the ground? On the dirt?
LILIKE: We nailed it in.
ANNE: How close is the grave to the water?
LILIKE: Come and check for yourself.
ANNE: Puckle's not ours to bury.
LILIKE: Yes, she is.

> *They sit for a long time.*
>
> *Eventually* RACHEL *enters.*

ANNE: Just ... sit. For now.

> RACHEL *sits. They all sit together.*
>
> *Eventually, the night sky gives way to the morning sun creeping out. And the rooftop garden and Collingwood now morph into the river.*
>
> ANNE *stands above the grave with a shovel.* LILIKE *and* RACHEL *are beside her, shovels in hand.*

RACHEL: Puckle. I freaked out. When I saw Lil and Anne that was one of the first times I'd been out in ages. And then they just scooped me up, they just seemed to know what to do with me. I'm sorry that I didn't know what to do with you.
ANNE: I'm no saint, Puckle. Remember our ritual? Calling Lizzie every evening, as we walked, leaving her messages? I was panicking, admittedly, because she never answered. I almost didn't meet Lil at the cafe. I thought, 'Oh well, maybe it's best you're gone, what would I have done with you, really, in the long term?'
LILIKE: You liked that custard song, Puckle girl. You liked my singing, didn't ya? It calmed you.
RACHEL: Rest in peace.
ANNE: Goodbye, friend.

> *They each heap in a last shovelful of dirt. As the sun rises, a huge frigging weird-ass friendship shrine seems to loom out of the earth, with a strange but comfortable glow.*

THE END

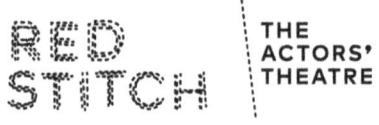

presents

SINGLE LADIES

18 MARCH–12 APRIL 2020

Playwright
Michele Lee

Director
Bagryana Popov

Dramaturg
Emilie Collyer

Set and Costume Designer
Romanie Harper

Lighting Designer
Rachel Lee

Sound Designer
Elissa Goodrich

Production Manager
Greg Clarke

Stage Manager
Rain Shadrach

Assistant Stage Manager
Lowana van Dorssen

Rachel – **Jem Lai**

Lilike – **Caroline Lee**

Anne – **Andrea Swifte**

Artistic Director
Ella Caldwell

General Manager
Fiona Symonds

Production Manager
Greg Clarke

Development Manager
Angelica Clunes

Front-of-House Manager
Penelope Thomson

RED STITCH ENSEMBLE

Ella Caldwell	Chanella Macri
Richard Cawthorne	Olga Makeeva
Jung-Xuan Chan	Dion Mills
Brett Cousins	Mollie Mooney
Jessica Clarke	Christina O'Neill
Kate Cole	Joe Petruzzi
Ngaire Dawn Fair	Dushan Philips
Daniel Frederikson	Tim Potter
Emily Goddard	Ben Prendergast
Laura Gordon	Clare Springett
Kevin Hofbauer	Kat Stewart
Justin Hosking	Sarah Sutherland
Darcy Kent	Andrea Swifte
Caroline Lee	David Whiteley
George Lingard	

BOARD

Anthony Adair (Chairman), Catherine Cardinet, Humphrey Clegg, Sieglind D'Arcy (Deputy Chair), Sophia Hall, Damon Healey (Treasurer), Tim Jacobs, Michael Rich, Henrietta Thomas (Secretary), David Whiteley

Red Stitch Actors' Theatre would like to acknowledge that we create our work on the lands of the Kulin Nations, and pay our respects to Elders past, present and emerging.

THANK YOU

This development and production of *Single Ladies* would not have been possible without the generous support of our donors and partners

KINDRED DONORS

The late Roger Riordan and the Cybec Foundation
Maureen Wheeler AO and Tony Wheeler AO
Sieglind D'Arcy
Anthony Adair and Karen McLeod Adair
Jane and Stephen Hains
Carrillo Gantner AC and ZiYin Gantner
Andrew Domasevicius and Aida Tuciute
Rosemary Walls
The Neff Family
John Haasz
Per and Ingrid Carlsen
Andrew Umney
Jane Thompson and Chris Coombs
Jenny Schwarz
Pamela McLure
Michael Kingston
The Kestin Family Foundation
Graham and Judy Hubbard
Linda Herd
Brian Goddard
Greg Day
Elise Callander
Margaret and Peter Yuill
Tony Ward and Gail Ryan
Ian and Grace Warner
Christina Turner and Lyle Thomas
James Syme
Fiona Symonds
Teri Snowdon
John Andrew Salvaris
Kaylene O'Neil
Mark O'Dwyer

Kate and Peter Marshall
Larry Abel
Janet Allen
Anita and Graham Anderson
Robin Blair and Chris Clarke
Ella Caldwell
MaryAnne Carroll
Julie and Ian Cattlin
David Creedon
Damon Healey
Jenny and Jock Jeffries
Peter and Liz Jones
George Klempfner and Yolander Klempfner AO
Edwina Mary Lampit (In Memorium)
Barbara Long

MAJOR PARTNERS

Creative Victoria
City of Port Phillip
Creative Partnerships Australia
Cybec Foundation
Lyngala Foundation
Malcom Robertson Foundation
Copyright Agency Cultural Fund
Besen Family Foundation
Sidney Myer Fund
The Myer Foundation

Rear 2 Chapel Street, St Kilda East, VIC 3183
http://redstitch.net/ | FB: @RedStitchTheatre | T: @redstitch
boxoffice@redstitch.net | 03 9533 8083

DIRECTOR'S NOTE

'I suddenly realised: everyone in this neighbourhood is about half my age! They couldn't see me.'

I came to Australia in 1973. One day we went walking, to get to know Melbourne. We walked from Northcote to the city, along the 86 tram line. Along the way, on Smith St, we looked into the windows of second-hand shops and furniture shops and shoe shops. It was Sunday and everything was closed. We were disoriented.

In the early 80s, I had my first cleaning job, in an artists' warehouse that overlooked Smith Street—the first of its type. Fitzroy had started changing. I used to ride along Smith Street late at night—no other bikes, few cars, and no people. I was always slightly scared and exhilarated by the grunge and the solitude. Then Collingwood and Fitzroy transformed before my eyes. It became the place to be, the place of artists, then architects, then it became unaffordable, cool and upmarket and crowded and political all at the same time. Melissa's, where I ate tiropita, has closed. Messina with its queues opened. If you stay in a place long enough it becomes a different place. A form of travelling by staying. And then you find yourself saying to young people 'This used to be here, that used to be there ...' And you can't quite explain what it was. It's moved on.

Anne and Lilike are of my generation. They are living in a fragmented world that is moving very fast, a world of ubereats, digital media, corporate speak. Rachel, who is young, is across all of that (or is she?). Then a dog enters their life, and everything shifts.

Michele has written a delightful play. A day in the life of Collingwood and three women, who make surprising discoveries about each other. *Single Ladies* is about public spaces, the invisibility of older women, and the need for connection and friendship. Women in a society that doesn't hold or support them, who, in different ways, are all struggling to find a place (literally and metaphorically) and to make connections to sustain them. And in amongst everything, always there, is the presence of the river— the Yarra.

I love that *Single Ladies* is a local play, about this moment in our society. And that it makes me laugh, and moves me.

My thanks to Michele Lee for entrusting me with her beautiful play, to Ella Caldwell for the opportunity direct it, to the wonderful actors Andrea Swift, Caroline Lee, and Jem Lai for their openness, humour and wisdom, and the terrific team producing, designing and stage managing this new work. Thank you to Peter Christoff and to La Trobe University Creative Arts, especially Dr Rob Conkie.

Bagryana Popov

WRITER'S NOTE

When I was about 17, my Year 12 Business Studies took us from Canberra to Melbourne. This was the late 90s, by the way. Chris and Jenny, our teachers, took us to iconic places. Queen Victoria Markets! Acland Street! Brunswick Street! I still remember seeing the decorated stone couches on Brunswick Street—we had nothing like it in Canberra. At one point we were taken to a hosiery factory, out in a manufacturing district. I'm sure that this factory is no longer around. Or if there still are hosiery factories here in Melbourne, I'm sure the retailers they supply are now small sustainable fashion labels promoting slow fashion. Chris and Jenny were trying to make a point with all of this. The connections between place, culture and commerce. I did really well in Business Studies because I over-prepared and over-studied. I don't know if I really understood, at the time, what they meant though.

I moved to Melbourne in 2004, and at that time it was still affordable for a lot of people in their 20s to rent houses in inner-city places like Fitzroy and Collingwood. Once I came back from an overseas jaunt and, temporarily homeless, I spent a week or so on my friend's couch. She lived on Napier Street, by a lane, where the real estate agent told the tenants to stick broken glass on the top of the fence to deter people from jumping it. And then just around the corner was Gertrude Street with its boutiques, its cafes, its galleries, its bars, maybe a social services agency, maybe an old milk bar. I would walk further, up along Smith Street, and feel buoyed by the contradictions of the gentrification that I participated in as a consumer, a diner, a would-be tenant. I have had this feeling, like many others, when I've travelled to the inner-city suburbs of other Western cities of comparable size.

There are many ways to participate in life in the city, in these urban boroughs. For women, there's a romance and a danger. There's found family, there's isolation. There are places to shop and eat, to reinforce a sense of 'I am this person, I am not that person'. Certainly coming to the big 'city' was where I was struck by the scaled-up heterogeneity in how people expressed themselves. When you think about yourself in relation to the city, and on your own, and as you age or as you fail or as you protest against change, that sense of expression and being has to shift.

The women in *Single Ladies* are women who live in Collingwood. They're pretty much strangers. Not in any way is that meant to admonish medium-density or modern living; more so just to state that that is what they are. I hope you enjoy getting to know them and them getting to know each other. I truly have.

Michele Lee

MICHELE LEE
PLAYWRIGHT

Michele Lee is an Asian-Australian playwright and theatre-maker working across stage, live art and screen. Her work is largely narrative-focused, in comedy and drama and explores stories of women, otherness and found families. She has been commissioned by Griffin Theatre Company, Sydney Theatre Company, Malthouse Theatre, Arts House, Next Wave Festival, Darwin Festival and Monash University.

Her play *Rice* won the 2016-17 Queensland Premier's Drama Award, the 2018 Victorian Premier's Literary Award, the 2018 Australian Writers' Guild stage drama award and was a finalist for the 2018 NSW Premier's Literary Award, Nick Enright Prize. Her play *Going Down* was a finalist for the 2019 Victorian Premier's Literary Award, Drama; a finalist for the 2019 NSW Premier's Literary Award, Nick Enright Prize; a finalist for the 2019 Australian Writers' Guild stage drama award and nominated for five 2019 Green Room Awards.

Michele has been awarded various residencies and fellowships and has assessed and judged for major awards and programs.

BAGRYANA POPOV
DIRECTOR

Bagryana is an award-winning theatre artist who works in an interdisciplinary way. She has collaborated with acclaimed professional artists, students and communities, working as director, actor, dramaturg and performance maker. She is interested in how artistic practice can speak about social and political reality. Much of her work has examined themes of relationship to place, refugee experience and war. Most recently she directed *Them* by Samah Sabawi, at Carlton Courthouse in June 2019. Previous projects: *Subclass 26A*, *Cafe Scheherezade*, *Sarajevo Suite*, *Of Cows, Women and War*, *Studies in Being Human*. Internationally, Bagryana has directed for the National Theatre of Macedonia, Bitola, and presented work in Finland and Bulgaria. Her PhD in performance (University of Melbourne) examined experiences of the Totalitarian communist era in Bulgaria. Bagryana has a passion for the plays of Chekhov and the way that they speak about the human relationship to our environment. She has directed *Three Sisters*, *The Seagull* and *Progress and Melancholy*, a dance-theatre version of *The Cherry Orchard*. Bagryana's site-specific, durational project *Uncle Vanya* transposed to the Australian landscape, co-produced with La Mama, was presented 2014-19 in Victoria, NSW and SA as part of Adelaide Festival 2019. Dr Popov is a theatre lecturer and researcher at La Trobe University. This is Bagryana's first project with Red Stitch, and she is excited to direct Michele Lee's beautiful new play.

EMILIE COLLYER
DRAMATURG

Emilie Collyer writes poetry, plays and prose. Her work mines the territory at the intersection of the personal and the socio-political and she is interested in bringing different forms into conversation with each other, including her developing practice as a dramaturg. Her work has most recently been published in *Plumwood Mountain*, *Slippage Lit*, *Australian Poetry Anthology*, *Cordite*, *Overland* and *The Lifted Brow*. Recent plays are *Contest*, *Dream Home* and *The Good Girl* which premiered in New York. Emilie's plays have won and been nominated for multiple awards including the Green Room Awards, George Fairfax, Patrick White and Malcolm Robertson. She is currently under commission with Red Stitch Theatre Company, via their INK program, and the script she is developing, *Super Perfect*, was shortlisted for the Queensland Premier's Drama Award.

JEM LAI
RACHEL

Jem is a Melbourne-based actor and theatre-maker. Last year she performed in *The Players*, a national education tour with Bell Shakespeare. In 2018 she co-directed and performed in *What If* (dir. Jessica Bellamy and Michele Lee) as a part of the ARTSHOUSE Refuge Festival. She also played *Mrs Marchmont* in the Melbourne Theatre Company's production of *An Ideal Husband* (dir. Dean Bryant). In 2017 she graduated from the Victorian College of Arts with a BFA in Acting and Theatre-Making. During her final year of VCA, she played Nina in the award-winning short film *Wild* (dir. Leticia Cáceres). She was also in the play *Never*, a work she co-created and performed in for FRISK at Melbourne Fringe 2017. In 2016, Jem was accepted as an exchange student into the Acting Bachelor at the Royal Conservatoire of Scotland (RCS), where she played Virgilia in *Coriolanus* (dir. Gareth Nichols).

CAROLINE LEE
LILIKE

Caroline has been working professionally as a performer for over 25 years. Most recently she has appeared in *Dance Nation, Escaped Alone, Rules for Living, Sunshine, Jurassica* and *Wet House* (Red Stitch); *'Night Mother* (Iron Lung Theatre); *The Exotic Lives of Lola Montez* (Finucane and Smith); *Conviction* by Zoey Moonbeam Dawson; toured regional Victoria with *Waking Up Dead* and toured China with *The Flood*. She has also performed in *The Trouble with Harry* (Melbourne International Arts Festival); *Waking Up Dead* (fortyfivedownstairs); and Bell Shakespeare's production of *Phèdre*. Film and television appearances include a main cast role in *Bogan Pride*, and roles in *Miss Fisher's Modern Murder Mysteries, The Dressmaker, Tangle, Winners and Losers, Satisfaction, Stingers, MDA, Halifax fp, Blue Heelers, Neighbours, Holidays on the River Yarra* and *Dogs in Space*. Caroline has won four Green Room awards and is also a well-known, and awarded, narrator of talking books.

ANDREA SWIFTE
ANNE

Andrea has been a Red Stitch ensemble member from 2008, when she first appeared in *The Pain And The Itch*. Past Red Stitch credits include *The Wide Night, on Ego, Fat Boy, Ruben Guthrie, The Princess Dramas, Stop.Rewind, Good People* and *Trevor* (Best Actress nomination, Green Room Awards). She has also worked for The Malthouse on *All Souls* by Daniel Keane and *Face to Face* by David Williamson. MTC productions include *Heart For The Future, Nana* and *Julius Caesar*. QTC/Malthouse co-production of *The Fortunes Of Richard Mahoney*, by Michael Gow and Dee and Cornilius's production of *Big Heart*. TV credits include *Offspring, Winners and Losers, Neighbours, Miss Fisher's Murder Mysteries, Tangle, Hollowmen* and *The Secret Life Of Us*. Film includea *Torn* and *Till Human Voices Wake Us*.

ROMANIE HARPER
SET AND COSTUME DESIGNER

Recent design credits include *Packer and Sons* (Belvoir), *What Am I Supposed to Do?* and *Equinox* (Deep Souful Sweats), *Australian Realness*, *Trustees*, *Good Muslim Boy*, *Little Emperors* and *Turbine* (Malthouse), *The Violent Outburst That Drew Me To You* (MTC), *Die! Die! Die! Old People Die!*, *We All Know What's Happening* and *Never Trust A Creative City* (Arts House), *Contest* and *Moral Panic* (Darebin Speakeasy, 2018), *Bottomless*, *This Is Eden*, *Resident Alien* and *Triumph* (fortyfivedownstairs), *Desert 6.29pm*, *Jurassica* and *Splendour* (Red Stitch) *Conviction* (ZLMD Shakespeare, 2016), *M+M* (Daniel Schlusser Ensemble), *The Sovereign Wife* (Sisters Grimm, NEON), *The Judgement* (LaMama) *META* (Malthouse Helium), *The Bitter Tears of Petra Von Kant* and *Bright World* (Theatre Works), and *Madonna Arms* (Next Wave). In New York she has worked with The Wooster Group, and co-designed Radiohole's *Inflatable Frankenstein* (The Kitchen, 2013). She has co-directed and designed *The Collected Works of Victor Bergman* (Fortyfivedownstairs, 2014) by The Family, and *Calamity* (NEON 2015) by ZLMD Shakespeare.

RACHEL LEE
LIGHTING DESIGNER

Rachel is an artist and lighting designer based in Melbourne and her hometown of Singapore. Design credits include Red Stitch's *Ulster American* (Brett Cousins, 2019), *She Is Vigilante* (Bridget Balodis and Krystalla Pearce, 2019), *Love/Chamberlain* (Cathy Hunt, 2019), *Forgotten Places* (Citizen Theatre, 2019), *The Three Graces* (The Anchor, 2019), *The Honouring* (Jack Sheppard, 2019) and *Blood Quantum* (Ngioka-Bunda Heath, 2019) at The Yirramboi Festival 2019, *World Problems* (Emma Hall, 2019), *Rent, The Musical* (Take The Mic Australia, 2018), associate lighting designer on

Moral Panic (Double Water Sign, 2018), *Fallen* (She Said Theatre, 2018), *Truly Madly Britney* (Stage Mom, 2019), *Baby Bi Bi Bi* (Flesh Coloured Panties, 2018), *Romeo Is Not The Only Fruit* (dir. Jean Tong, 2017-2019), *Tandem* (Gravity Dolls, 2018) and *Bread Crumbs* (On The Fence Productions, 2017) and several 2018 Melbourne Fringe productions, including *Born to Achieve: A Little Sister Proves Her Big Sister Wrong* and *Lou Wall's Drag Race*. Throughout this year, she is in development for works as part of Sydney Gay and Lesbian Mardi Gras, AsiaTOPA, Red Stitch, Theatreworks and Next Wave. Rachel has completed internships with Nigel Levings, Nick Schlieper and Paul Jackson. She was also part of 2019 Melbourne Theatre Company's Women In Theatre Program and works closely with Western Edge Youth Arts (WEYA) on their various productions.

ELISSA GOODRICH
SOUND DESIGNER

Elissa is a composer and percussionist with an abiding interest in collaborative artforms. Elissa's soundart works have featured in Centre de Cultura Contemporanea Barcelona, MADATAC (Spain), Soundwaves, International Lightworks Festival (UK), Sonori Sguardi, Tempo Reale (Italy), Melbourne International Arts Festival, International Sonorities Festival of Contemporary Music (Northern Ireland) and in audio-visual collaborations at the Museum of Otago, Pataka (NZ) and Tempo Reale (Italy), *Double Dialogues* (UK/Aus.), *Punctum* (Aus.), Traverse International Video-Art Festival (France), Museum of Networked Art (Germany). Two-time nominee for Australian Jazz Work of the Year, Elissa's *Forgotten Songs of Flight* in duo with cellist Caerwen Martin performed at National Opera Center (NYC, US) (2017). Alongside Elissa's soundart *Between Footsteps* (Heide MOMA), her *Gene Tree Project* continues in partnership with St Martin's Youth Performing Arts Centre. Elissa is composer-recipient of APRA AMCOS Art Music Fund for *Gene Tree* (2018-2022).

RAIN SHADRICH
STAGE MANAGER

Originally from Spain, Rain started her career as a stage manager in the UK in 2019 by shadowing stage managers from West End musicals including *Everybody's Talking About Jamie* (The Apollo Theatre), *Come From Away* (Phoenix Theatre) and *The Lion King* (The Lyceum Theatre). She has recently moved to Melbourne where she's worked as a stage manager for Goodfellow Theatre Company's production of *A Midsummer Night's Dream*, *Scarborough*, Encore Theatre Company's production of *The Witches* and TBC Theatre's production of *Rust* for the Midsumma Festival.

LOWANA VAN DORSSEN
ASSISTANT STAGE MANAGER

Lowana is a recent graduate of the Victorian College of the Arts where she completed a Bachelor of Fine Arts (Production) in Stage Management. Whilst at the VCA, Lowana interned with The Melbourne Theatre Company and Chunky Move, whilst also working across a variety of disciplines; dance, theatre and music theatre. Her final year saw her production manage *Body* by Sue Healey and co-stage manage the inaugural theatre-maker graduates in their final VCA performance, *Swim Between The Flags*. Lowana was also thrilled to work for the Wilin Centre on *Fan The Flames* in 2019. Outside university Lowana has stage managed two seasons of *Trio of Dips: Love Me Tinder* and *Night Creatures: Electric Loneliness* at the Butterfly Club. Lowana is a proud member of the MEAA.

RED STITCH ACTORS' THEATRE

Red Stitch Actors' Theatre is Australia's leading actors' ensemble.
Established in 2002, we exist to advance the vitality of Australian theatre by nurturing artists and promoting integrity in our craft.
The ensemble of actors and creatives who comprise our company endeavour to produce the best in contemporary playwriting from around the world, to enrich the craft of acting and script development in this country, and to sustain a unique organisational model—one that puts artists at the centre of its practice.

We play a vital role in the development and presentation of new Australian works through our unique INK playwriting program, and offer opportunities for theatre-makers at all stages of their careers to hone and develop their craft. With a national reputation for the quality of our work, Red Stitch remains at the forefront of contemporary Australian theatre practice.

www.redstitch.net

Red Stitch's INK program is proudly supported by:

www.currency.com.au

Visit Currency Press' website now to:

- Order books
- Browse through our full list of titles including plays, screenplays, theory and reference/criticism, performance handbooks, educational texts and more
- Choose a play for your school or performance group by cast specs
- Seek performance rights
- Find out about performing arts news and sign up for our newsletter
- For students: read our study guides
- For teachers: access free curriculum information and teacher notes

We are also on Facebook and Instagram (@currencypress). Join the conversation!

The performing arts publisher